Marc Bekoff

with illustrations by

Michael J. DiMotta

Animals at Play

rules of the game

For Rosalind— With
all best wishes—
much peace!
Love—
Marc

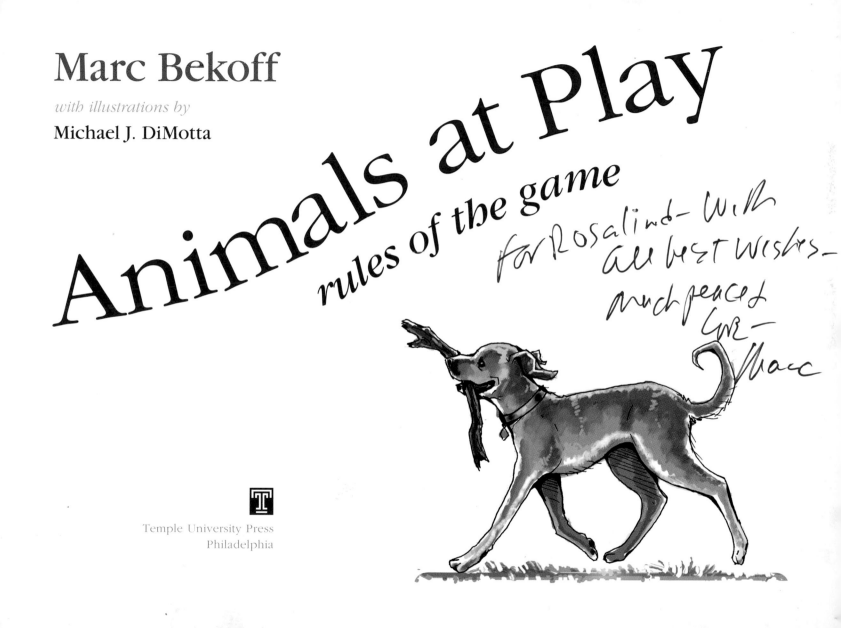

Temple University Press
Philadelphia

Temple University Press
1601 North Broad Street
Philadelphia, Pennsylvania 19122
www.temple.edu/tempress

The publisher gratefully acknowledges the Found Animals Foundation, Inc.,
for its generous support of the publication of this book.

This book is printed on acid-free paper for greater strength and durability.

Library of Congress Cataloging-in-Publication Data

Bekoff, Marc.
Animals at play : rules of the game / Marc Bekoff ;
illustrations by Michael J. DiMotta.
p. cm. -- (Animals and ethics)
ISBN 978-1-59213-551-6 (cloth : alk. paper)
1. Play behavior in animals--Juvenile literature. I. DiMotta, Michael J. II. Title.
QL763.5.B45 2008
591.56'3--dc22   2008022140

2 4 6 8 9 7 5 3 1

Printed in China

Two dogs chase each other. Pounce. Wrestle. Bark. Bite.
What do these actions mean?
Are they playing? Are they fighting?
How does one dog know what the other dog wants?
Do they have rules? Do they cheat?
Look closely. Pay attention. The animals do.

Do animals play?

Many animals play—from rats to ravens to coyotes to sea lions. Like people, the young ones mostly play—with each other, with older sisters and brothers, with cousins, and with adults.

Grownups play too, usually with their young, but only when they aren't busy hunting or protecting the group.

Why do young animals play?

Their play is for exercise, gaining strength, and developing muscles for when they grow older, so they can travel long distances and run fast. They are the prey and must run away to avoid being a meal. Or they are the **predators**, trying to catch their meals.

Playing is also a time for learning. Learning how to fight, hunt, and mate—social skills they need when they become adults.

In their games, young animals learn the rules of living in a group—and how to communicate or "talk" with each other. They learn to cooperate and play fair.

Life in the wild can be tough. It's even tougher when you're alone, so play helps to create bonds and a sense of community.

And . . . playing is fun!

Predators *are animals who eat other animals for their meals.*

Because playing can look like fighting—biting, shoving, chasing, and pouncing—animals have to let others know that they want to play and not fight. Most animals communicate or show their playfulness through specific actions that they all recognize or know.

As they play, animals communicate or "signal" what's allowed and what isn't. Their playmates pay close attention to make sure that all the pouncing, shoving, and wrestling stay playful and don't change into fighting.

Animals even follow rules!

1. Everyone has to want to play.
2. Everyone has to cooperate—they work together—to keep the game from becoming fighting.
3. Everyone needs to communicate and pay attention to each other's movements, sounds, and smells.

Many **species** begin to play in different ways. But the one thing that they have in common—they first *ask* their friends if they want to play.

Species is a word for a group of animals who share certain traits in common and are able to have young like themselves.

Coyotes, wolves, jackals, and foxes play like dogs because they're in the same **family, the dog family** or **Canidae**.

Look closely. You'll notice a similar pattern with all dogs at play.

Shorty wants to play, so he approaches Cody. He stops in front of her, crouching on his front legs, his rump in the air, wagging his tail.

This is a play bow. It's how Shorty asks Cody to play.

If Cody is facing away, Shorty barks once or twice to get Cody's attention, to say, "Hey, look at me."

This is a friendly bark. It's not like the barking that goes on and on, which is a warning bark.

Once Cody knows that Shorty wants to play, Shorty will dash away, hoping to start a chase.

Cody gets to choose whether she wants to play or not. If she does, she will chase him.

Watch carefully. You'll see Cody bow quickly before she pounces on Shorty. This bow tells Shorty that the jump is playing. The play might be rough, but Cody doesn't want to hurt Shorty.

Sometimes you'll notice dogs stop wrestling and move away from one another. They could be tired, needing a break before they chase again.

Or one of the dogs might feel that the game became too rough.

Maybe Cody bit too hard and shook her head wildly from side to side, which is aggressive, not playful. Shorty will back away, stopping the game. If Cody wants to keep playing, she will approach Shorty and bow, asking Shorty if he wants to play again.

Now, it's up to Shorty to choose.

*The word **family** is a major subdivision for classifying animals or plants. The dog family Canidae includes wolves, jackals, coyotes, foxes, and domestic dogs.*

Imagine if elephants played like dogs—running, jumping, chasing! The forests and savannas, or grasslands, would be in shreds. So might the elephants!

Elephants don't play quickly. Their play looks like a dance.

They move slowly toward each other, swaying their heads and trunks until they are standing side by side. Then, they rest their tusks and trunks on the other's back, still swaying with each other. They might wrestle with their trunks, but are careful not to use their tusks.

They might repeat this "dance" for hours—moving away and then moving toward each other, swaying together.

Sometimes their play includes hosing each other with water if they're in a lake or river.

Elephants' play is calm and graceful.

Unlike elephants, rats move fast. Young rats love to chase, wrestle, box, and jump on one another when they play.

The difference between playing and fighting is the spot on the body where a rat "attacks" a friend or an enemy.

When playing, a rat uses his snout to gently rub another rat's neck. That rat would use different moves—twisting away or running—to stop his friend from touching his nape, or neck, which is part of the game. It's what you'd do to stop your friend from tickling you.

But in a fight, a rat bites the rump of another rat!

Depending on whether you're a friend or an enemy, you'll either have your neck rubbed or your rump bit.

Many felines—such as house cats, cheetahs, and bobcats—ask others to play by approaching one another, usually from the side. They arch their backs and then often jump into the air. Sometimes, instead of jumping, they tilt their heads and paw at the ground. Cats also retract—or bring in—their claws when they play, so they don't scratch their friends.

Lions, though, begin their play with a play bow—like dogs, coyotes, and wolves.

When gorillas or chimpanzees want to play, they stroll up to each other with a loose, bouncy walk, called gamboling. Their shoulders and head sway from side to side. One may hit the other lightly on the shoulder and then run away as though saying, "Chase me."

Their playing is like contact sports—they wrestle and roll on the ground. They "mouth" each other—gripping one another with their mouths, like dogs do.

They even use a play face that resembles smiling. They might pant softly. Why? To show that they want to play, not fight.

Polar bears also lumber toward each other with a bouncy gait. They push, shove, or touch a shoulder to express that they want to play. Often they wrestle. They hold on to one another as they roll in the snow or on the ice, doing somersaults together.

Very tough and strong animals—like gorillas and polar bears—use their walk to communicate that they want to play. Long before they are near each other. This way, there's no confusion that it's a time to play, not a time to fight.

Squirrels chase each other up and around trees, from branch to branch, across telephone wires, and along fences. They're called **arboreal** animals.

Rhesus monkeys of India and black-and-white Colobus monkeys from Kenya chase, wrestle, and play hide and seek on the ground with members of their own kind. Rhesus monkeys also swing through the air on branches—their own monkey bars—to chase one another through trees.

But Colobus monkeys are like acrobats! They leap fifty feet from one tree to another. How? Branches are their trampolines!

Arboreal animals live in or spend most of their time in trees.

Not all animals use gestures—like the play bow or the elephant's swaying—to show that they want to play.

Short-tailed voles are small rodents who live in woodlands, scrub lands, and hedgerows. They have a gland on the back of their necks that produces a "play **pheromone**," which is a special chemical or odor. This smell signals playtime—it's like a play bow.

One whiff—and it's time for fun!

Yellow-bellied marmots wrestle, chase, and punch when they play. Their playing is bouncier than fighting.

How can you tell they're not fighting?

When they play, they're silent. When they fight, they growl.

Mammals aren't the only animals who play. Ravens chase each other in the sky. They also play alone. They use sticks, twigs, leaves, pebbles, and food as toys.

In the winter, they don't need a sled. They slide down steep mounds of snow on their feet. Then they fly or walk to the top of the mound to slide down again.

A pheromone is a chemical that causes a behavior in other members of the same species.

Mammals are warm-blooded vertebrates with skin usually more or less covered with hair. Vertebrates are animals with a backbone. Mammals feed their young with milk produced by mammary glands. Humans are mammals.

Who doesn't dream of being a dolphin or seal swimming through the ocean? But do they play?

Yes, sea mammals also play. Dolphins, sea lions, and harbor seals chase and roll together in the water.

Dolphins can't change their facial expressions or wag their tails to show happiness, anger, or fear.

Instead, to communicate that they want to play, dolphins swim toward each other from the side. If one dolphin swam head-on toward another, that would mean that the first dolphin might be looking for a fight.

Imagine a dog in the water. Take away the legs and give her flippers and a strong tail. Now, instead of a bone or a stick in the mouth, imagine a piece of kelp, or seaweed.

That's a sea lion starting to play. A sea lion carries the kelp in her mouth. Then, she swims away from her friends, inviting them to join in. If they want to play, they'll chase her.

A harbor seal waddles to a friend. He leans his chin or head on the shoulder of another seal—in the same way elephants ask their friends to play.

The seals begin playing by wrestling or chasing. They might go into the water to continue their fun.

Sometimes in the middle of playing, excitement takes over.

Did you ever whack a friend by accident when playing tag instead of tapping her on the shoulder? Or throw a ball too hard to your younger brother?

You didn't mean to hurt your friend or your brother. When that happens, you apologize.

Animals also become very excited when they play. Sometimes, they don't realize how strong they are compared to their friends. A nip turns into a painful bite. Shoving becomes ramming, knocking a smaller friend over onto his back.

What do they do?

They apologize, of course, just like you!

Dogs, coyotes, and wolves use the play bow to apologize. Remember when Cody bit too hard and shook her head wildly from side to side? Shorty backed away from her. To apologize for her bad behavior, Cody bows, her rump in the air, her head down to the ground. Shorty forgives her. Playtime continues.

An elephant accidentally nicks his friend with his tusk as they sway together. The hurt playmate steps away.

To apologize, the other elephant steps close enough to gently touch his friend with his trunk. Or maybe using his shoulder, he leans into his friend. They look as if they are holding each other up.

The touching is the apology.

To show he accepts the apology, the hurt elephant steps forward. He then lays his trunk gently on his friend's back. They begin their dance again.

Imagine gorillas, or other **primates**, wrestling for fun. One gorilla bites her friend too hard. The hurt friend stops and moves away. She squints her eyes and tilts her head, as if asking, "What happened? I thought we were playing."

The gorilla who bit walks over to her friend. She puts her hand on the other's shoulder to apologize. She might even groom her friend to show she cares and didn't mean it.

The grooming or the touch on the shoulder lets the friend know that she's sorry and won't do it again. Feeling reassured now because she knows it's safe—that the bite was an accident—her friend is ready to play again.

Although expressed differently, these apologies are similar.

1. The hurt animal stops playing and steps away from the more **aggressive** friend. Because the animal was hurt, he's unsure of what his friend will do next.
2. The friend who pushed or bit moves toward his friend. He then performs an apology (the play bow, grooming, or touching), promising that the accident won't happen again.
3. The hurt friend accepts the apology and begins to play again.

The most fascinating part of the apology is the trust between the two animals. Even though it could be unsafe, the hurt animal allows the friend to come close enough to touch—to make the apology

Safety and trust are part of apologizing.

*A **primate** is any member of the biological group (called an "order") that contains all the species related to lemurs, monkeys, and great apes, including humans.*

***Aggressive** describes a kind of behavior. An aggressive animal threatens or even tries to fight another animal.*

Did you know that some animals lie and cheat?

Tom, a young coyote, asks Jack to play. He agrees. Tom pounces hard. Jack backs away, confused by the roughness.

Tom, then, performs the play bow. Jack accepts the apology. Playtime continues.

But again, Tom pounces, hurting Jack. Jack steps away. Tom bows.

Jack may or may not play again because Tom cheated. Tom asked Jack to play when he really wanted to fight. He even bowed to apologize, but he wasn't honest. He did mean to pounce hard, for he did it twice. He lied.

Animals will forgive an honest mistake. But, like you, they don't like cheaters and liars. A coyote might give a friend two chances, but maybe not a third.

What happens to a liar like Tom? You probably guessed—no other coyotes will play with him because he cheats. This outcome is even worse than having no friends to play with.

The other coyotes will avoid Tom. If he goes near them, they will walk away. They might even walk around him. Basically, they ignore him.

Finally, Tom will leave the pack because he no longer has a place there. Living alone in the wild isn't easy. His chances of survival will be very small.

For animals, there are two ways to cheat or lie.

1. After hurting a friend, an animal apologizes, but then hurts the friend again.
2. One animal asks another to play, but bites too hard and tries to dominate, or take over. This isn't playing. It's fighting.

If you have little sisters, brothers, or cousins, you know how to play with them. In a race, you don't run too fast. When playing catch, you don't throw too hard. During a board game, you help your younger sister take her turn.

It's only fair. You're stronger, quicker, and bigger.

When adult animals have enough food and don't need to worry about predators, they enjoy playing with their kids.

But how do they stop from squashing the little ones?

They hold back, which is called "self-handicapping."

When grown-up red-necked wallabies—cousins of kangaroos—box with younger wallabies, they punch gently or just slightly touch. They don't push hard or move too quickly. The older wallabies make playtime last longer by not frightening or hurting the little ones.

An older wolf allows a pup to "dominate"—to be more powerful. Pretending to be weaker, slower, and clumsier than the young animal is called "role reversal."

If an adult used his full strength, the younger animal would get hurt and not want to play.

You're now a beginner **ethologist**, a zoologist who studies animal behavior.

Go out! To your local park. Your backyard. Your neighborhood.

See the dogs. Spy on cats. Sneak a peek at the squirrels outside.

You have the skills to know when they're playing, apologizing, and trusting one another.

Notice how animals catch "the play fever"! Once animals see others playing, they join in the fun, sharing the excitement and joy.

Pay attention to how people play. Are they giving signals to show that they want to play? Do adults change their behavior when they play with children? How do people know that apologies are real?

Or just watch animals chase, wrestle, and tumble!

Have fun watching animals play!

Acknowledgments

I am indebted to Susan Wallach for patiently listening to "lectures" about animal behavior and for all the hard work she did to make this book a reality.

~~~~~

About the Author

Dr. Marc Bekoff is an ethologist and well-published author who travels the world, speaking about animals and working with children. He taught biology for 32 years at the University of Colorado in Boulder. Marc co-founded Ethologists for the Ethical Treatment of Animals (www.ethologicalethics.org) with Jane Goodall. He also works closely with children as part of the Jane Goodall Institute's Roots & Shoots program.

Marc has won many awards for his scientific research. The Bank One Faculty Community Service Award honored Marc for the work he has done with children, senior citizens, and prisoners.

Marc has written for such magazines as *Ranger Rick*. He's also appeared on Animal Planet and National Geographic Television.

You can learn more about Marc, animals, and ethology on his web site, http://literati.net/Bekoff.

In the series, **Animals and Ethics**, edited by Marc Bekoff

~~~~~~~

Author: Marc Bekoff

Editor-in-Chief: Janet M. Francendese

Editorial Development: Susan Wallach

Production Director: Charles H. E. Ault

Illustrations: Michael J. DiMotta

Design and Composition: Kate Nichols

This book was composed in ITC Garamond
and was printed and bound by Everbest Printing Co. on 100# matte paper.